T0099863

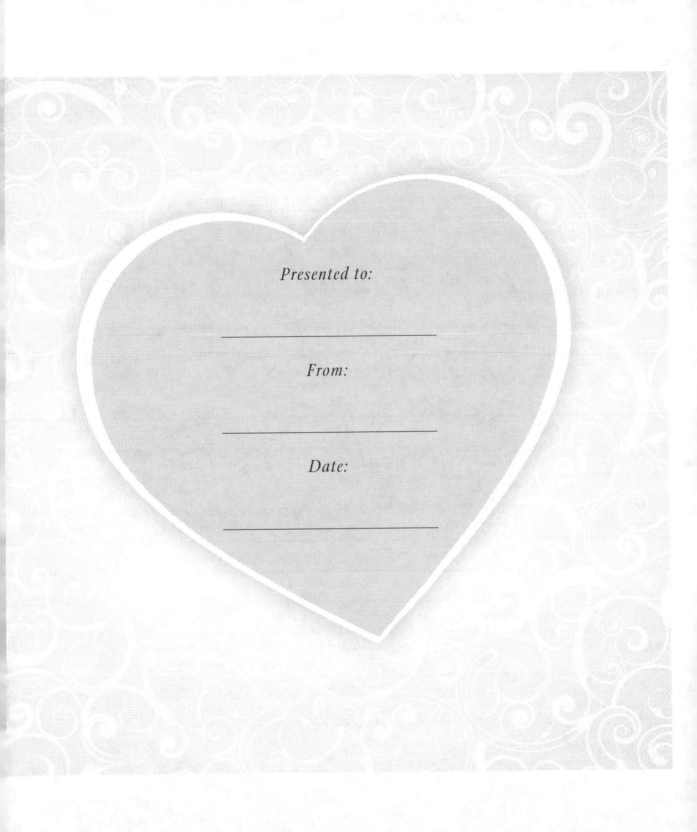

Presented to:

_____

From:

_____

Date:

_____

For there is no friend like a sister,
In calm or stormy weather,
To cheer one on the tedious way,
To fetch one if one goes astray,
To lift one if one totters down,
To strengthen whilst one stands.

<small>CHRISTINA ROSSETTI</small>

kisses

from a

Sister's
Heart

Heartwarming Messages
That Express a Sister's Love

HOWARD BOOKS
A DIVISION OF SIMON & SCHUSTER
New York   London   Toronto   Sydney

Our purpose at Howard Books is to:
- *Increase faith* in the hearts of growing Christians
- *Inspire holiness* in the lives of believers
- *Instill hope* in the hearts of struggling people everywhere
  Because He's coming again!

Published by Howard Books, a division of Simon & Schuster, Inc.
1230 Avenue of the Americas, New York, NY 10020
www.howardpublishing.com

HOWARD   *Kisses from a Sister's Heart* © 2008 by Dave Bordon & Associates, LLC

All rights reserved, including the right to reproduce this book or portions thereof in any form whatsoever. For information, address Howard Subsidiary Rights Department, Simon & Schuster, 1230 Avenue of the Americas, New York, NY 10020

ISBN-13: 978-1-4516-4327-5

10 9 8 7 6 5 4 3 2 1

HOWARD and colophon are registered trademarks of Simon & Schuster, Inc.

Manufactured in the United States of America

For information regarding special discounts for bulk purchases, please contact: Simon & Schuster Special Sales at 1-800-456-6798 or business@simonandschuster.com.

Project developed by Bordon Books, Tulsa, Oklahoma
Project writing and compilation by Christy Phillippe in association with Bordon Books
Edited by Chrys Howard
Cover design by Greg Jackson, Thinkpen Design

Scripture quotations marked NASB are taken from the *New American Standard Bible®*, copyright © 1960, 1962, 1963, 1968, 1971, 1972, 1973, 1975, 1977, 1995 by The Lockman Foundation. Used by permission. (www.Lockman.org)

INTRODUCTION

A kiss. It's short. Sweet. And packed with love. That's what *Kisses from a Sister's Heart* is all about. Each page of this book is a message straight to your heart from mine, filled with joy and gratitude for the wonderful sister that you are. As you read, I hope you'll discover how very much you mean to me— now and always.

Every good thing given and every

perfect gift is from above . . .

JAMES 1:17 NASB

1

You, my dear sister, are one
of God's greatest gifts to me.

You understand me better than anyone else—my silly side . . .

my serious side . . . .

my cheerful side . . .

my grumpy side . . . and
everything in between.

We have our own special language—

the goofy look, the raised eyebrow,

the sister smile,

the hug that says,
"Things are going to be okay."

We know all of each other's secrets

but we'll never tell!

That's just the way we are—
you and I.

Sticking up for each other.

Having fun together.

Staying close to each other.

Taking care of each other.

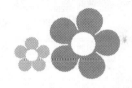

And you always seem to know just when
I need—a second opinion . . .

a latte · · ·

or an ice cream cone . . .

an encouraging phone call . . .

a box of chocolates . . .

or a drive in the country.

No one has more fun together!

Through all the
lemonade stands . . .

and the backyard explorations . . .

lazy days at the pool . . .

the pillow fights . . . .

and the pillow talks . . .

the giggle fits . . .

and collapsing in the grass . . .

you've always been my
favorite friend.

Even now that we're all grown up,

when it's time for a chick flick,

or a good cry,

or manicures and pedicures,

or just some good, old-fashioned
retail therapy,

you're the one I call.

We've shared everything:
Barbie dolls . . .

puppies . . .

picnics ...

and vacations . . .

lipstick . . .

85

clothes . . .

and shoes.

We've even shared the same room.

But the greatest thing
we've ever shared is our
love for our family

and our love for each other.

You're always there for me.

You cheer me on

and encourage me to reach
for the stars.

In fact, I believe in me because you do.

I know that no matter
what the future brings—whether
happy times . . .

or sad times . . .

whether sunny days . . .

or cloudy ones—

we'll always be
close.

We are two peas in a pod.

We are cut from the same bolt of cloth.

We are sisters!

I am so thankful that God gave me
wonderful you!

LOOK FOR THESE BOOKS:

Kisses of Comfort

Kisses of
Encouragement

Kisses from a
Friend's Heart

Kisses of Love

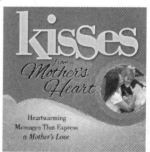

Kisses from a
Mother's Heart

HOWARD BOOKS
A DIVISION OF SIMON & SCHUSTER
New York   London   Toronto   Sydney

Printed in the United States
By Bookmasters